VERMONT FARM AND THE SUN

by Constance and Raymond Montgomery

Photography by Dennis Curran

Vermont Crossroads Press   Waitsfield, Vermont

This book is a children's easy reading book aimed at three groups of children: the preschool child looking at the photographs, the beginning reader who connects the photos with the text, and the remedial reader who sees all ages of children in the pictures and is encouraged to read.

International Standard Book Number 0–915248–01–8
Library of Congress Catalog Card Number 75–29688
Printed by The Stinehour Press, Lunenburg, Vermont
Copyright © by Constance and Raymond Montgomery, 1975
All rights reserved
Vermont Crossroads Press, Box 333, Waitsfield, Vermont 05673

The sun is hot.
The sun makes plants grow.
The sun is energy.

A farm collects energy from the sun.

Plants need sun, water, and soil to grow.

8

Plants use the sun and keep its energy
in their leaves, their stems, and their fruit.
Plants are storehouses of energy.

A farmer collects the energy of the sun in the plants.

The food grown on farms is energy for us.

Life on a farm moves with the sun.

The hay is cut.

The tractor takes it to the barn.

Joe and Jim pitch hay in the barn.

Hay is food for the cows.

The cows are hungry. They eat the grass
in the fields and the hay in the barn.
Cows change grass and hay into milk.

Goats eat the same food that cows do.

They give us milk, too.

Ann pets the goats.

The black puppy on the farm drinks milk from his mother.

John shows the puppy to the goats.

The puppy gives the goat a kiss.

Life on a farm means fixing tractors and ploughs.
Joe helps his father fix the machines.

The tractor runs on gas. The earth stored the energy
of the sun in plants that died years ago. Dinosaurs
lived in those days. The dead plants became oil.

People found the oil under the ground.

We use the energy in the oil to run machines.

Machines make some jobs easy to do.

Many jobs are done by hand.

These farmers are building a silo.

Grass is cut in the summer and fall and put in silos. The cows eat this food all winter long. The silo is a storehouse of energy.

We eat the food from the farm.

We work and play in the sun.

Vermont Farm and the Sun is a children's easy reading book aimed at three groups of children: the preschool child looking at the photographs, the beginning reader who connects the photos with the text, and the remedial reader who sees the older children in the pictures and is encouraged to read. Although it is aimed at a second grade reader, it can be used by both older and younger children.

This book stresses the concept of the earth as a solar collector. A farm is a specialized solar collector transforming the sun's energy into plant and animal fibre and tissue, making it available for human consumption for growth and to sustain life. The concepts of the transformation and conservation of energy inherent in the book are important ones for children to begin to understand.

Constance Montgomery, the co-author, was a writer and editor at *Newsweek* and *Vogue* magazines. She is the author of the children's book *Vermont School Bus Ride* and the adult biography *Hemingway in Michigan*. Having graduated from Sarah Lawrence College, she received her M.A. in English from Columbia University.

Raymond Montgomery, the co-author, has been involved in teaching, education research, and curriculum design. A graduate of Williams College with graduate study at Yale and NYU, he served as Assistant Provost of Columbia University. He developed a high school social studies program entitled *The Energy/Environment Game*, which is currently being used nationwide in schools.

Dennis Curran, the photographer, is a photo journalist who lives in Warren, Vermont. He is the New England Motocross editor for *Cycle Sport* magazine and a ski photographer in the winter. Dennis won the first prize in the scenic category and two honorable mentions in the U.S.A. E.U.R. European Army Photo Contest.